MW00935440

Praise for The Clearing Process...

I have been a student of metaphysics and New Thought for over 25 years. Recently I experienced a particularly challenging emotional situation in which all my years of spiritual practice confused me. Pat was gently able to guide me back to my spiritual foundation by leading me to go deeper into the mystery, and allowing my inner guidance to resurface. Her wisdom and the Clearing Process are a life raft for me.

Rita McLain. Forest Knolls, CA

Rev. Pat Palmer has written a powerful book that anyone can use to clear out emotional wounds. The Clearing Process is a step by step process that enables one to feel and then release toxic emotions. The result of using the process is freedom and renewed sources of energy and joy.

Nevin Valentine
Certified Relationship Coach Imago Couples International

I LOVED your book Pat! It is very clear and easy to follow and I KNOW how powerful this kind of work is. I am going to recommend it to my spiritual group!

Rev. Grace Koch

Thank you for reminding me of my own vibrations; the ones that influence the way in which I relate to my own loved ones. I have been seeing that this is totally about the vibes I'm putting out there! I am so grateful for the work we've done together!

B.B. Detroit, MI

This book is incredible - it's like GOLD!! Such straight forward help! The writing is very clear-- and makes sense. I'm really impressed with the structure and order of it. There are people out there who are really READY to do this work, and this book will be their Bible. You and your Soul wrote this book!

Carina Reisberg, Rife Therapist

The Clearing Process

... for Conscious Living

Rev. Pat M. Palmer

The reader is encouraged to see "The Clearing Process Workbook" which accompanies this original guidebook. The Workbook provides the step-by-step structure that makes it much easier to do this powerful processing on one's own.

Further information is available at the website www.clearingprocess.com.

For in personal contact, write to Rev. Pat Palmer at clearingprocess@icloud.com to arrange for counseling either in person, or via computer.

ISBN: 978-1-300-21796-1.

Cataloging Publication Data

1. Self-Help   2. Spiritual   3. Transformation   4. Healing

Dedication

This work is dedicated to my mentor
and friend Rev. Liz Claire, who loved
me until I could love myself.

It was Liz who first listened to me
deeply, until I could listen to my self.

It was Liz who showed me the power
of being with my feelings, until I knew
that is the only way to heal at source.

Thank you Liz for beginning my
clearing process... my conscious living.

Table of Contents

Table of Contents, continued

INTRODUCTION

Many people live lives of desperation; some beginning with the circumstances of birth, and some because they inadvertently continue to create their pain. Many more others live lives of what they think of as 'ordinary' frustration, riding the roller coaster of emotional highs and lows; feeling powerless to create the joy they believe could be theirs, and which is their natural state.

Occasionally breakthroughs occur. A person discovers a way to change from living in reaction to life's events, to a more heightened awareness for living consciously. They learn to turn toward that which seems to be the cause of their problems, rather than turning away from it. They begin to see the power they hold over their own circumstances. Life begins to work - very well.

The Clearing Process is one such pathway. It is a self-therapy, yet can be most effective when learned with a trusted other. This book provides excellent guidelines for you to do the inner work on your own. You are also given information to contact a Clearing Process therapist.

To benefit from the Clearing Process one must hold, or at least be willing to consider holding, a philosophy of life that provides a foundation for conscious living:

~ Do you have a sense that there is a power and a presence greater than your individual self, which has your good as Its agenda?

~ Can you believe that your deeper Self chose to be born into your family specifically to set the stage for you to carry out your life's purpose?

~ Do you think it is possible that every element of life is aware and responsive - to you?

If you are still reading, perhaps the Clearing Process is for you. Possibly this approach to life will give you the surprise of dissolving that which you do not want - like it did me. Maybe, once you surrender to fully 'being with' your truth, this process will amaze and delight you too.

The Clearing Process is surprising. Over the years I've received phone calls and emails from clients who were doing the process at home and needed reminders about how to do it. I finally realized that it would be helpful to put it all down in writing. This book is for them - and for you!

It's also an expression of my desire to contribute to the healing of the world, one person at a time.

Pat Palmer
October 16, 2012
www.clearingprocess.com

PART 1

The Power of the Clearing Process

There are countless forms of therapy now
available to those of us open to changing
ourselves. As you reach a place in Mind where
you become ready to let go, and ride the journey
of spiritual and emotional growth, exactly what
you need for that process will be drawn
to your attention.

Part I describes the birth and development of the
Clearing Process. A bit of my healing story, and
those of several other clients, will illustrate some
ways others have used the Process.

Part I is also an overview of the background and
rationale for this approach to healing one's life.

5

CHAPTER 1
My Story

Here I was, 42 years old, in my second marriage and the most miserable I had ever been in my life! On the outside, it all looked good; I had a nice car, a home on 200 acres outside of Gainesville, Florida, and my own successful business. My two lovely and wonderful daughters from my first marriage were teens and growing up to be good people, as far as I could tell. They had been opposed to my marriage, and I had not been able to understand why. I remember telling the girls, and my sisters, "Finally, I found a man who is going to take care of us and life will be much easier!" I loved him so much. And of course I did not know what love was.

The real story was gruesome! When we were at home alone at night, as the drinking progressed, my husband became verbally and eventually physically abusive. I had sent both of the girls away; the 13 year old to live with their dad, and the 15 year old to stay with my one friend. I was afraid for the younger one's safety, since she was so rebellious, and for the older one's sanity. I thought maybe having them gone would improve the marriage too, since I was trying everything I could think of to make it work.

I was educated, with a master's degree in Counseling and 60 graduate hours toward my doctorate in Psychology. I thought I knew what I was doing. I tried so hard! My belief was that if I just could find a way to be good enough, he would love me and I wouldn't need to be in fear.

As I share that story, it seems like it happened to another person. My life is so different today! It began for me with surrender; I got that my best efforts were not working. I realized that I did not know what to do!

Out of desperation, I began attending a spiritual center, and had just begun to look at life as a spiritual journey. Then my minister and mentor, Liz, began inviting me to tell - to tell her, and myself - the truth.

I began to let go of talking about who had done what to who, and to instead get in touch with my feelings. Gradually, I discovered that the terrible fear that incapacitated me in my marriages was exactly the same as I had felt as a child!

My dad was a heavy drinker and would rage and hit my mom whenever he came in from another bout. She was fearful, and helpless, yet determined to stay with him. My sisters and I hid under our beds and cried when we were little. Later, as teens, we became creative in finding ways to protect our mom from being hit. Fear was always just around the corner. We never knew when...

As I opened spiritually and emotionally, I discovered that in addition to the fear, which I could remember, there had also been the aloneness, and helplessness, and the anger which I had repressed and never even admitted to. I was still holding these toxic emotions repressed and didn't even know it. Those were the energies creating my life, over and over.

As I began to see how I had been unconsciously setting myself up, I became open to healing. Relevant practices began coming to me, and I used them to begin my own clearing.

Gradually I incorporated other teachers' healing techniques and my own understanding into what I now call the Clearing Process. It has evolved to become an amazing vehicle for seeing one's life clearly, and more importantly, for transforming those emotions which keep blindness and stuckness in place.

The Clearing Process leads to emotional freedom!

In the twenty-five years since the realization that my life wasn't working, I have not only healed my own life, but have had the joy of facilitating the healing of emotional issues for many others as well.

I was my first client. I learned this effective approach to healthy living through my own gradual emergence from a repressive, pain-filled past. I learned about emotional healing the only way someone really can, through experiencing it myself.

CHAPTER 2
The Greater Story

The Clearing Process can be learned as a self-therapy. The rewards of the work are immense! Not only does the presenting problem dissolve, one learns how to apply the technique to other emotional challenges that inevitably arise in the years ahead.

We develop confidence that crises will fade away as we learn to be with ourselves in awareness and self-love. We become less buffeted about by what others do or what happens to us. Life becomes much more gentle, and happy.

Clearing is the process of working with our own soul. We are not in this particular body and social circumstance by accident! Our Soul Self chose our root family as perfect for the journey we were being born to take. And that family, that birth experience, was perfect for creating the conditions to stimulate the very process we are now in - breaking through the cocoon into our own greatness!

For most of us, infancy and childhood experiences generated a need to repress some of our feeling responses. That need to keep those intense emotions unconscious stems from the survival mandate to have the love of our parents no matter what!

We don't even realize we are still holding that intense energy. It is telegraphing itself to our universe, repeatedly creating opportunities to come out into the open. But we get stuck thinking our feelings are about whatever the current crisis is; attributing the intense reactions to that as cause.

The Clearing we seek comes from telling ourselves the truth of how we feel. By immersing ourselves in our "now" experience, without blame, we allow the stuckness to reveal itself. By being fully in the present, we open to the past and relate with it as we could not then.

We then gain the ability to authentically and mindfully feel our emotions. It is the simplest and yet the most powerful healing modality yet discovered. We become empowered and free.

CHAPTER 3
The Process is Surprising

In the beginning, The Clearing Process is challenging because it is so different from the way the majority of people think about why and how things happen. In fact, as a therapy, it is contrary to most counseling approaches.

Many psychiatrists, including Freud, Jung, Adler, and their followers, developed theories and treatments which did not include remembering and reliving childhood abuse. People have spent years in psychoanalysis learning how to talk about emotions, but not able to feel them.

Most forms of therapy help people learn how to minimize what happened to them, and to forgive their parents/perpetrators in order to become well. Popular psychology and spiritual teaching sometimes focuses on letting go of bad emotions, not healing through them. We are encouraged to feel good to create good. And we have been in a prozac revolution for many years now.

The shadow side of the information revolution, with our growing desire for speedy solutions, is that we have less tolerance for staying with anything - let alone our emotions. We want everything to have a quick fix.

For that reason, much emphasis is on trying to change our external behaviors. Of course those behaviors are due to a much deeper, unconscious urge/motivation, which is creating (over and over) the same problem situations in order to heal itself. To change any one situation does not heal that repressed need.

The purpose of the Clearing Process is not to assist in putting band aides on problems to only have those wounds open up again later. The power of Clearing is that it dissipates the buried feeling at the source.

Clients are not encouraged to DO anything differently. It won't matter whether a person does or does not change what they are doing. The whole focus is on how one feels. Behaviors transform as a natural result, once we are no longer being directed by the spiritual mandate to attend to un-experienced emotion.

> I remember how my two sisters, coming from the goodness of their hearts, spent many hours around my dining room table, trying to help me figure out what to DO about my marriages!

> In the first marriage, I had left my husband five times, taking our young children along. Each time I returned saying he 'needed' me.

The second marriage was even more painful, as life tends to be if we don't 'get it.' My dear advisors were no more capable than I of seeing my need to set myself up for pain over and over.

They believed, as did I, that if I just did something differently the situation would change. We did not realize the power of the drive within me to heal the past - to process the fear and underlying anger and contempt I was still holding.

Loving attention to the childhood feelings (that have been repressed in the very cells of the body) heals the old wounds, and one's vibration changes. People and experiences which resonate with that old energy are no longer drawn to us.

We are no longer incapacitated by formerly threatening situations. We can easily handle them now. Our creativity and joy increase, as the psychic energy which was engaged in keeping old negativity repressed is freed. We begin to choose relationships which empower us.

After my initial healing work, I became involved in a 12-step program, with the mandate 'no relationships for the first year!' I was fascinated, as time went on, to observe the kinds of men who previously attracted me!

I saw that I had been drawn to men who were ego-centered and needing to have power-over, like my dad had been in his abusive treatment of his family. Now, I no longer had any problem saying NO.

We also find that when other negative experiences occur in future life, as always happens, we again use the Clearing Process which we have learned. We readily make the connection with how this new emotion has been resident in us since childhood, give it full attention, tell the truth about the pain, and it too dissolves. Life is good!

After some time, I allowed myself intimate relationships again, and I continued to heal the old wounds. For me, it happened in layers; first the fear, then the anger, then the contempt - much of which I had never been in touch with before, and yet had held repressed in me since childhood.

CHAPTER 4
Pre-requisites

I find that the first pre-requisite for success in the Clearing Process is to have a spiritually-grounded awareness of how life unfolds. It is invaluable to realize that Spirit, or whatever one calls the creative source of being, is always supportive of Its creation - meaning us.

If we know that, then we can actually come to view each experience as a doorway to greater joy in living. Only then can we stop resisting what is happening, and use it.

Secondly, we need to accept that the cause of any situation is never outside of oneself. Consciousness and only consciousness is source - both individual consciousness and our part in the shared consciousness of the human race.

Everything else is secondary cause; i.e. cause only from the perspective of how things appear to be. The challenge is that most of the world, including those well-meaning friends who try to help us the most, is convinced by how things appear to be.

CHAPTER 5
Bigger than I Realized

In researching for this guidebook about the Clearing Process as a contribution to the field of emotional healing, I have come to understand that the far-reaching extent of emotional woundedness is actually an enormous problem for the whole world.

Because it is part of the spiritual unfolding of human beings to unconsciously set up ways to feel whatever we had to repress as children, we are continually involving others. I, for example, was led to keep choosing relationships which gave me reason to feel afraid; my model was my mom and she was very co-dependent and fearful. I also chose relationships in which I would fear my partner.

For some, it is tremendous anger that they are driven to keep creating ways to express. The abuse they encountered as children generated huge RAGE, which they were forced to keep inside. As adults, they find reasons to feel that rage, and to punish other people with it as though they were the cause.

The work of Alice Miller (*Breaking Down the Wall of Silence*) is renowned for her exploration of this issue. She gives examples, and discusses and documents the consequences of having people in power who have not dealt with their childhood issues; who are carrying rage, and use their power to hurt others. "Drug addicted and alcohol addicted pay with their lives; those addicted to power - tyrants - pay with the lives of others."

For the most part, society is not cognizant of this unfolding of events. (I had not previously heard it discussed.) Badly abused children are usually unaware of the existence and righteousness of their childhood feelings!

According to Miller, 78% of high school students in France in 1989 stated that the beatings they had received as children were necessary and just. Among all of the brutal dictators in the world, there is not a single one who did not approve of the abuse he himself once received.

It is accepted that we have genocide, war and stockpiling of weapons to maintain power. The cruelty of tyrants is attributed to genetic factors or psychic illness. Also according to Miller, "The mistreatment of children is the worst crime against humanity; it insidiously creates generations of deformed personalities."

On the other hand, according to Miller, people ruled by tyranny are those who became convinced as children that God was acting through their parents - for their own good. Just as we have difficulty extricating ourselves from abusive situations if we don't understand our drive to heal through them, people who live in totalitarian systems cannot free themselves from tyrants. They need help from the outside world, and international law to protect them.

Miriam Greenspan (*Healing Through the Dark Emotions*) maintains that there is a profound relationship between dark emotions and the state of the world... "The idea of healing emotions for collective well-being is an idea whose time has come."

Our inability to be aware of and tell the truth about our feelings is at the bottom of our blindness to the current destruction of our planet as well.

Adam Trombly, of Project Earth, stated in his interview in Wildfire magazine, "People aren't educated emotionally, spiritually. It's literally as if feeling has stopped in human culture.

"People are numbed, in shock. It's like a body... If you stick your hand into a fire, pain signals are sent to the brain. The human body, as it stands right now, is disassociated from its feelings; it doesn't feel the rainforest being cut down, the underground nuclear explosions.

"Yet, I am convinced we do feel it...so we've got to start realizing what it is we're feeling because the impulse has to get from the hand to the brain and to the heart, so we can pull the hand out of the fire; so we can take corrective action - do a different ceremony than we're doing. The earth has been profoundly destabilized by the withdrawal of feeling."

Today we're at a turning point. Just as I was in my life, when the pain had become so great that I had to wake up or go under, our human race is at that point.

There are many effective actions now finally being taken by those who realize the earth's crisis. In addition, we must also find ways to tell the truth to ourselves about the fear we have for the earth and our own survival. We must feel it.

CHAPTER 6
Supplementary Resources

My teachers along the way were Rev. Liz Claire (my beloved Science of Mind minister) Michael Ryce (*Why is This Happening to me Again?*) Colin Tipping (*Radical Forgiveness*) and John Ruskan (*Emotional Clearing.*) I am indebted to each for their wisdom, their books and the encouragement they provided me in the early years.

Additional inspiration came from Eugene Gendlin and Ann Cornell (*Focusing*) J. Konrad Stettbacher (*Making Sense of Suffering*) Miriam Greenspan (*Healing Through the Dark Emotions*) and the work of Alice Miller. I also recommend Brandon Bays (*The Journey*) and Byron Katie (*The Work.*)

I continued to build on the approach I had used on myself, integrating my own discoveries. I began by facilitating Clearing at first for relatives and friends, and then by holding small group seminars and workshops. I gradually developed a large practice.

The trust and the healing work of many clients have also significantly contributed to what this clearing modality now offers.

I have great respect and love for all who entrusted me with their hearts and hopes.

PART II

The Clearing Process Itself

In Part II you'll be invited to apply the Clearing
Process concepts to yourself, in order to gain a
deeper awareness of how it can work for
you personally. The symbol ℭ℟ is used
to note exercises which will help you to
deeply enter the process.

Questions follow each chapter.   Use your journal
to respond before progressing. Please wait until
you expect to have a few minutes of
uninterrupted time.

Writing down your inner reactions may allow you
to actually experience the clearing of an old issue
even while reading about the process
for the first time !

CHAPTER 7
The Underlying Philosophy

As with any self-help approach, the more faith we have in the process, the easier it is to embrace. It works better for us. If you are in agreement with the following premises, we are on the same page. If you are not, please consider whether you might want to try them on for size - fake it 'til you make it - so to speak.

1) Life is perfect!
I have everything I need to serve my unique purpose in this lifetime.

2) Spirit lives as me, and is supportive to the extent I turn toward It.
It is said that if I take one step toward Spirit, Its entire power turns toward me.

3) My root family was chosen by my Soul Self to foster in me the challenges I need to evolve.
Nothing is accidental; all serves my divine journey.

4) Any emotions I wasn't allowed to feel as a child, I may still carry in me in a repressed state.
I don't have to try to remember them; they come up in me in my response to situations that upset

me. The persistent problems in my life today come from those very same emotions I repressed!

5) One way to catch that the present is being dictated by the past, is that the intensity of the emotion is usually much greater than would normally be warranted by the present.
When one little thing happens that is reminiscent of the past, if it is touching upon something we haven't healed, the whole file containing that feeling in our subconscious gets activated. So we may react way out of proportion to what seems to be the cause.

6) Understanding the wounding is not enough to heal it; that is the booby prize.
Striving for understanding appears to be an intelligent reaction to problems. And when it seems like we understand, it feels rewarding. Unfortunately, that reward is only a booby prize, because only the surface changes. No deep healing can occur through only the intellect.

> I came to understand that I always accepted the anger directed at me because that's what my mom had always done. I had fear of the other person's anger, but I was helpless to change my reaction because she had been helpless. Still, this understanding did not change anything. I still drew angry men into my life.

Now that I have gone deeper than just understanding, and have fully experienced and healed my pre-existing fear, there is NO anger directed at me anymore.

7) To again encounter my wounding, I am drawn to situations which will cause those same emotions.

It is all selective perception. Our perceptions are governed by what we expect to see. We have learned to subconsciously expect life to be a certain way. So we unconsciously expect to encounter situations and people that will bring up those old feelings. In fact, we may not even notice events and situations which do not eventually lead us to feel that negative.

8) Blaming or trying to change the people or circumstance does not heal the wounds.

If I get rid of a person or circumstance that seems to be cause, another will take its place.

9) Only attending to those emotions will allow them to dissipate.

Trying not to feel them, or avoiding those situations that cause them, is not effective.

10) I don't TRY to make something happen; I invite it to make itself known to me.
Our deep self wants to support us in healing; we just need to reassure the ego that we can handle whatever comes up. We are adult now.

11) By gently encouraging myself I will begin to remember.
My ego releases its protective barriers and allows my subconscious to inform me.

12) It is not necessary to confront the person who seems to be the cause; this work is with myself.
In most cases, if I were to tell the person about my upset, they would react strongly. They might take it personally. They might try to help me feel better. Dealing with their reaction would likely distract me from my own process. However, I may choose to let them know I am getting in touch with some old pain from the past, and that I am doing the processing around it.

How I deal with others will change on its own later, as I become clear.

> Later in my life, at the spiritual center I then directed, a volunteer was taking control of an event I was preparing. She was telling me what to do, and taking over preparations for the celebration. I felt an inner response of

RAGE; it was quite out of proportion to her action.

Then I got that my feeling was actually about my dad - how controlling he was. I never had a voice. As I sat there breathing and feeling the rage, my hands felt frozen in place and it felt like I couldn't move them; I just stayed with it. The anger totally disappeared.

Thank God I had not raged at her; I knew she was just the catalyst.

13) The Clearing Process is not about forgiving!

Premature forgiveness can cover up the feelings that are wanting to be explored and heard. What is necessary for healing is the opposite of forgiveness - the recognition of what was done to me, and the expression of the rage to myself.

True forgiveness comes spontaneously, after the truth has been recognized and experienced. Then the pain is no longer present.

14) I already Know what to do; I just have not been able to access it.

When it seems like I don't know what to do about something, it's because the unfinished emotions around that issue are acting like a layer over my own intelligence. When I have felt the emotions fully, I will see clearly. I just need to dissolve the barriers to knowing.

15) The present circumstances of life then change of their own accord.
I am no longer drawn to situations and people who bring up this emotional pain. The psychic energy I was using to keep the feelings repressed is now free to create.

I AM HEALING THE PRESENT - BY FEELING THE PAST REPEAT ITSELF IN ORDER TO BE HEARD!

Journal Experience:

I have seen Spirit act in my life when...

What comes up for me about my life purpose is...

One situation that I feel intensely about today is...

CHAPTER 8
The Childhood Phase

A. Human beings strive for self-preservation.
This instinct is operative particularly in children, since they don't know how to think in a self-protective manner.

As Alice Miller says, an abused child "must totally repress the mistreatment, confusion and neglect it suffered. If it were not to do so, it would die. The child's organism could not withstand the dimensions of this pain. Only in adulthood do other ways of handling our feelings become available to us."

Some children were able to cry when sad, laugh when happy, yell when mad; most of us were shushed, pushed away or told to be quiet. According to Miller, parents have three styles of repressing: ignoring, stopping or shaming and punishing. That's how they teach children to control their feelings. At the time it is happening to us, we believe it is right to beat children. We don't even know there are people who would never use violence against their children.

According to Stettbacher, a child's main need is to be respected. Then they have the courage to state their needs.

When Kate asked for therapy, it was because she was so discouraged about the poor relationship she had with her children. She felt like she was always walking on thin ice because they got mad at her so frequently. Her daughter had not spoken to her in over a year.

Kate's childhood family was well-off financially. Appearance was important to them, particularly to her mom. When they were around others, Kate was treated politely and bragged about. However, when they were home, Kate was frequently in trouble for saying the wrong thing, or not having her dress clean enough, or forgetting to do something she had been told. Her mom spoke to her harshly and abusively and often told her father to beat her for perceived wrongs.

Kate grew up in fear of offending others, and right up until we began the Clearing Process she actually believed that she had deserved to be treated so badly. Through clearing she was able to begin to think well of herself and to expect to be respected. Her relationships with her grown children transformed!

B. The biggest cause of suffering for children is not having anyone to tell.
When children are physically intimidated, they are afraid to call their parents into question.

However, childhood repression doesn't have to happen if there is someone to assure the child that what is happening is not right; a witness who can validate the child's experience by acknowledging their pain. If that did not happen, we don't trust our memory about what really was done to us.

In later years, we may develop the habit of laughing or making light of our past when we talk about it. Perhaps we preface the memories with saying, "It wasn't that bad." This approach is a lie; a way we use to support our ego's effort to still hold those feelings secret.

> David was very worried about losing connection with his daughter, and his two-year old granddaughter. Their conversations were pleasant as long as everything went well, but whenever there was the slightest problem, if David mentioned it, his daughter would fly into a rage! He told me he could not talk to his daughter about anything! It was becoming intolerable.
>
> When David came for therapy, it became apparent that his childhood family didn't do negative feelings at all. If anything bad happened no one talked about it.
>
> When his father was in the hospital, no one ever told him where his dad was, or what was

wrong or why he didn't come home. Even when his dad died, his mom did not tell the family. It was left to an aunt to tell the children.

When David was asked at school about his dad, he didn't know what to say. He simply did not know how to respond, and became very confused. He resolved this lack by becoming numb to his own feelings. He had never learned to acknowledge them, let alone deal with them.

Not until we really began exploring his painful relationship with his own daughter, did he realize how deprived he had been as a child, and how much pressure he had been under to never talk about anything bad.

Picture the vulnerability of a child at three. That's how we were. All we wanted to do was laugh and love! However, once we start talking about it, and feel listened to, we begin to trust our memories. We get a freedom to remember more and more. We gain strength and passion in our recounting of the way it was!

C. We must not minimize the severity of the emotion we buried within us as kids.

The feelings were intense! And over the years since, they stay the same intensity and do not mature with us. When an emotion has been repressed, it never gets processed through healthy expression. It has the same intensity as any childish emotion.

To successfully navigate the healing process, the emotions need to be re-experienced with that same intensity. As Alice Miller states, "It's not enough to just tell the facts of it. We must have the emotional awareness of what it felt like to be so abused. We must empathize with the child we once were."

And we can do this! We think we can't remember about childhood, but in truth every smell, every sight, every emotion is indelibly imprinted in our subconscious. When we let ourselves imagine how it might have been (by becoming empathically in touch with whatever we CAN remember) the subconscious guides us to envision it truly.

> Jeannie had fallen deeply in love at age twenty-five. However, her boyfriend was ready to split up, claiming he could not bear her insecurity. Whenever he did not call enough, or was late coming home, she would go into a panic of worry that something was wrong.
>
> When Jeannie's mom and dad split up and he moved out, she had been eleven. Her mom fell apart, so she had no one to support her understanding of the situation. Meanwhile

her dad moved in with his girlfriend and her children who were about the same age.

Jeannie readily remembered that she retreated from the whole situation; she told me she began spending most of her time with friends and was home as little as possible. What she had not remembered was how terrified she was that her dad was lost to her forever; that he would love his new family more than her.

Through Clearing, she was able to vividly recall conversations with her father and mother, and to let herself clear the fear and sadness of abandonment she had repressed so deeply.

D. As an adult now, we can be the advocate of the child within.

We can be the voice of the child who has never really been silenced. We can also pretend to be the parent - one who listens compassionately to the feeling the child voice was never able to express.

Often we find, as we listen over time, that deep patterns become apparent. The formerly repressed emotions can stem from even our parents' childhoods, and from their parents as well. Toxicity is usually a family pattern that gets passed down the generations. Now we have the opportunity to say, "the buck stops here!"

Donna asked for help because she realized that again she was in a relationship with a man she could not respect. Both of her marriages, her long-term affair, and her current lover were all men she ended up having contempt for in one way or another.

She had been so careful who she chose this time, yet she saw that she had again been blinded by 'love.'

As we discussed Donna's feelings for her dad, it became apparent that she had indeed had contempt for her father. She said there were many reasons, and she chose to share one in particular with me.

As the oldest child, she had often sat talking with him in the evening, listening as he drunkenly recounted the day's problems at work. By serving in this role, she allowed her mom to have some peace and sneak off to bed, before he could pick a fight with her.

What Donna could not admit however, was how much disgust she felt about him as they sat for hours at the kitchen table together. Further exploration revealed that her mother had also had contempt for her husband. In fact, Donna was able to find out that her

39

mom's parents divorced because the mother had caught her dad in their bed with another woman.

Donna got to experience not only the truth of her own feelings as a child, but to act out the feelings of her mom and her grandmother. She came to a place of clearing the contempt she had been holding for men.

Journal Experience:

A challenging circumstance in my childhood was...

The person who really listened to how I felt was...

One thing from childhood I've never told anyone is..

CHAPTER 9
The Six Steps of the Clearing Process

The Clearing Process is recommended for whenever you have a situation in your life that is upsetting, especially if you have experienced that particular uncomfortable emotion previously.

The objective is not to feel better; rather it is to BE WITH your emotions in such a way that you realize them more fully and more intensely. This conscious attention will allow them to clear. They've been heard. They no longer will exert a powerful, subliminal force of attraction in your life.

CR PAVE THE WAY FOR YOUR HEALING...
As you begin this work, you can increase its effectiveness by preparing the way within your own self. This is most easily done through self-talk and affirmations such as "I am on the path to healing this area of my life; I am an adult and can handle whatever comes up; It is okay for me to tell the truth to myself."

Use strategically placed Post-its! These kinds of reminders reassure the subconscious and pre-dispose the ego to soften its protective stance over your subconscious.

It is highly recommended that you do the steps of the Clearing Process in order, with attention to the detailed description of the approach.

Stories from clients, illustrating healing different emotions and challenging situations, are presented at the end of this section. The names and some details have been changed to protect privacy.

It sometimes happens that when we really begin accessing our deeply held, repressed emotions, there is some resistance from the ego self. For example we might find ourselves depressed, or tired, or feeling disconnected, or catch a cold. Keep on reassuring your self that this is okay to do; that this is the right path to take; that healing is happening.

Journal Experience:

When I consider doing this clearing work, I feel...

One situation in my present life that I would like to shift through Clearing is...

STEP 1: Open to a heightened AWARENESS of your uncomfortable feelings. ACCEPT them fully.

It may be difficult to become aware of feelings if you do not usually think about how you feel. In fact, some people answer the quest for feelings by beginning with the phrase "I think." Usually that means the mind has gotten involved, and will not reveal actual feelings.

When we accept feelings the way they are, they can change. When we try to change them, they don't. Feelings don't go away by not looking at them, like people want to believe.

In our culture, people tend to turn away from the hard emotions like fear, sadness, etc. The last thing many people want to do is go through them, even if going through them would lead them to unimaginable gifts on the other side. We are taught to endure, deny, bypass, avenge and escape our negative emotions.

And the more we lock up our feelings, the more we're convinced we could not deal with them if they come up. Fear and resistance to them make them so much scarier and bigger.

▶ **We can't heal what we don't feel !**

Trying to have patience or trying to be forgiving, can actually be an unconscious effort to avoid our feelings. These efforts forestall the healing process. What emotions really want is to be attended to! The moment we become aware of a negative feeling, we must embrace it. In fact, make it even more intense!

▶ **We must turn toward our feelings, not away from them.**

Lie down in a dark room and invite your deeper mind to reveal to you how you are feeling about the situation. As each feeling makes itself known. whisper to it, "I see you and I accept you."

We may also find ourselves asking WHY something is happening. Exploring 'why' gives us the illusion that we are doing something intelligent. Actually, trying to figure out WHY is a major distraction put in our way by the ego. The ego is trying to save us from feeling what it thinks our inner child cannot survive letting itself feel.

The truth is we already know the answer to WHY! The problem is happening because it is in response to an old wound we are holding that is vibrating its frequency out to our environment, and attracting situations to provide a reason to feel that way. That is the WHY! Refuse to go down this road in the mind! It is a dead end!

▶ **Ask not WHY do I feel this, but rather HOW do I feel?**

Cornell, in the process called Focusing, suggests we approach the feelings from the attitude of not-knowing - being curious about them. "There are parts of us that want to be heard, without judgement, without criticism, without advice." Clearing is going to come from hearing what we don't know - not what we already know! As we repeatedly ask HOW we feel, and insights arise in us, we will be inspired to remember and to connect the dots - seeing the truth.

℞ Use the Non-Dominant Hand Exercise to get in touch with the subconscious mind. Draw a line down the middle of a blank sheet of paper. On the side of your dominant hand, write a question like, How do you feel? On the other side, use the hand you don't usually write with to respond to the question in cursive.

The effort of writing the letters occupies the conscious mind, so that the ego self drops its guard that usually keeps scary feelings repressed. The words that come up may be quite revealing. Then keep repeating

the same question, until no further response comes up.

Another pitfall is the temptation to focus on what to DO about the situation, instead of just becoming aware of your feelings. That also is a distraction by the ego. It is trying to keep us from feeling how bad it is to not have anything to do to make the pain go away.

Yet when we were little, that's how it was; there was nothing to do to make it better. That's the feeling we want to re-create, in order to dissolve it.

▶ **There's nothing to do, only something to feel.**

ജ **Whatever you think you need to do to make a situation better, don't do it! Rather IMAGINE doing it and see how that feels. The resulting old fear or anger, etc. will be brought up to be felt. Attend to it and accept it fully as the truth of how you feel.**

By refusing to be distracted by thinking about what to DO in the situation; by resisting the temptation to figure out WHY it's happening; by inviting the help of your deeper Self in a way that is curious rather than urgent, you begin the process of telling your self the truth, without judging yourself - the first step to Clearing.

Journal Experience:

How do I feel about this?

How difficult is it for me to admit that I feel those emotions?

On a scale of 1 to 10, how much can I accept these intense feelings in myself?

STEP 2: NAME and describe your feelings precisely. Visit them where they reside in your body.

The emotions we are experiencing in our painful situation are the key to opening and clearing the woundedness of the past. You never need to be in this situation again.

Even though the people and circumstances are different as we repetitively play out this issue in our life, the feelings will always be exactly the same. So the doorway to healing is really getting in touch with those feelings.

℞ The best way to begin a relationship with your feelings is to relax. Find a quiet space, breathe consciously, have an awareness of your body, and don't be in a hurry. Give it time. You may want to have your journal or a tape recorder available.

Brandon Bays, in *The Journey* provides an excellent sample list of possible emotions: anger, rage, frustration, anxiety, loss, depression, betrayal, feeling inferior or unworthy, low self-esteem, jealousy, sadness or hurt, sensitivity to criticism, loneliness, abandonment, grief, despair, fear of the loss of a loved one, fear of failure or being judged, etc.

▶ **The easy answer isn't it!**

Sometimes we have developed a reaction to thinking about our past that becomes habitual. For example, a person who always cries when speaking about their childhood may have learned to allow crying because it is more acceptable than the repressed underlying emotion, which could be rage for example.

Go deeply into whatever is there inside! Don't assume. Bays suggests we ask "and what is underneath that?"

The labeling of the feeling doesn't need to be definite or decisive yet. Stay open. It's more that we want to BE WITH it, in a way that is alert and listening to our own wise Self.

℞ If you've ever had a child, or helped name a child, you may recall the process of seeking the best name. You probably tried out aloud the name being considered, and then checked inside of yourself to see if that felt right. That's how we can most effectively begin to deeply BE WITH our feelings in a respectful, curious way.

Ann Cornells' book *The Power of Focusing* provides the best roadmap I've seen for allowing this seeking to contribute to the healing process. She says that our feelings want to communicate with us. They want to be heard. In fact, the desire by our feelings to be heard - and thereby healed - is so strong that it has led us to unknowingly create the entire situation.

▶ **We can trust our feelings and our body to lead us to the whole issue.**

From Cornell: "Continue to sense for just what description would fit perfectly... 'No, that's close, but it's not exactly that. Let's feel that some more...yeah, it's more like this...' When you find the description that fits your experience, you'll feel a satisfying sense of rightness."

ᘒ Another way to name your feeling more intimately, is to seek an analogy that captures it exactly. For example, "the feeling is like trying a walk a tightrope strung between two buildings" or "it is like a squirrel going round and round on a wheel and getting nowhere."

As you get a sense that you are in clear relationship with your emotion, ask yourself where you feel the emotion in your body. All repressed emotion is literally trapped in our cells.

It is well known that emotional pains have exact counterparts in our physical self. We can use the language of the body to form a deeper communication with what our inner child is wanting to tell us.

▶ **The body is eager to help the healing Process. It has been waiting to be asked!**

By letting your inner eye scan your body from top to bottom, you will be led to where the feeling resides. Bring in the power of your imagination to provide a way to listen to the emotion more empathetically. Your very attention is what will allow it to inform you.

ଔ Imagine that your Spirit Self is looking at the body sensation representing your feeling. See how big an area it takes up; what color it is; if it is hard like concrete or soft like a marshmallow; if it has a temperature; if it is heavy or light, etc. Imagine if it had a face what would it look like.

These kinds of imaginative observations allow a by-passing of the ego-intellectual mind which had been trained to keep these feelings unconscious. Imagine that Spirit is actually speaking to the body-representation of your feeling, asking it why it is there; what it wants from you; how it feels. etc.

What happens as you develop a sense of knowing your feelings is that you open to them. You fully accept them as having been in you since you were very young and you set up the possibility of being informed by them.

▶ **Don't mind that you don't yet know what the feeling is about. That will come of its own accord later.**

As you continue with the Clearing process, you will allow your emotion to lead you deeper and deeper into your own wisdom.

Journal Experience:

As I allow myself to BE WITH my painful emotions, they seem like they are...

An analogy/picture that might describe this feeling is...

Where is this emotion located in my body? It looks like.......and is......and......and......

When I ask it what it has to say to me it replies...

STEP 3: Ask yourself WHEN in the past you have felt exactly the same way.

Our Spirit Self is leading the way by repeatedly inviting us to finally heal what we have been carrying repressed in ourself most of our life. We unconsciously create new opportunity after new opportunity to finally tell ourselves the truth about the intensity of the emotion, and process it this time.

▶ **As Brendan Bays describes this process, "Source is relentless in its desire to heal you."**

We always will find, when we can intensely go into our feelings and accept them, that we have experienced exactly the same reactions with other important people in our life over the years. How we respond to our current challenging situation is exactly the same as we have felt and thought before; probably many times during our life journey.

> I remember whispering to myself when I was in pain in yet another relationship, "I can't believe he's throwing me away like this!"
>
> Then I was shocked to realize that I had despairingly said that same thing several times before, about other men in my life. That was a huge awakening!

The circumstances were different each time. Yes, the people involved were probably different ones. The only thing that is exactly the same is the way you felt when it all happened.

So don't get trapped believing that it's only in response to this current situation that you feel this way.

CR   Make a list of other times when you have had the exact same feeling.

The earliest time always turns out to have been with our parents or other care-givers when we were little. We didn't have the words then, or the courage, or opportunity to express them. And as these feeling situations recurred in life, we didn't recognize that they were the same ones happening again!

Michael Ryce addresses this so well in his work *Why is this Happening to me Again?!*

CR   Follow the trail of feelings back to its source to identify the earliest memory you have of this feeling. Find and get out photos of your self as a young child, and of your home and family as it was then, to help you remember.

▶   **Go for it!**

Journal Experience:

I felt this same way as I do now when...... and also when......and when......

The earliest time in my life I felt this was when ...

What happened then was...

STEP 4: OWN your life! Refuse to believe that anyone or anything outside of your self is causing how you feel now.

We think that it's our kids' behavior that makes us angry, or the high cost of living, or our spouse's unfaithfulness. Everyone agrees that cause is outside of us, and that's how it appears.

Actually, it's only our perception that makes it appear that way. All people, places and things in our life are there in response to our unique vibration.

▶ **We are the source; people show up to be pawns in our drama!**

Life is a spiritual process which brings people into our lives who are perfect for us. Sometimes they bring us joy and we are thankful for them. Sometimes they enable us to feel whatever we've repressed so we can heal it.

▶ **Everything begins within.**

People we resonate with are drawn to us in response to our long-held, repressed emotion. That emotion is subliminally vibrating and transmitting this message out to life: "Do it to me again! I need to release this emotion and maybe this time I'll be able to own it and take responsibility for it!"

CR **Refuse to listen to your mind going over and over why he or she is to blame; why you are right in blaming them. Say "Back Off" to your mind when it is going on and on. Tell your mind, "Thank you for sharing" and stop the cycle. Say to yourself, "There is something else going on here and I am going to find out what it is!"**

Those we love are the ones who most effectively bring up our pain. That's because they are the ones we let into our heart space; who can activate feelings of love in us comparable in intensity with what we felt for our parents as children.

We are divinely guided to let a person get close enough to resonate the same emotions our root family did. In fact, those are the people we fall in love with! Our loving relationships are perfect for bringing up stuff that is old and ready to be healed.

▶ Don't kill the catalyst!

CR **Notice, when you're upset at someone you care for a lot, if the intensity of your feeling is high; perhaps even higher than if someone else had done whatever they did to**

you. **The truth is that the feeling they are resonating in you is probably much more intense than you are letting on. That's because it's not really about them.**

Journal Experience:

I felt like it was his/her fault I feel this way because it appeared that...

I had an inkling that this might happen when...(but I ignored it.)

STEP 5: BE WITH your feelings intensely, directly experiencing them.

People do lots of work on healing - but often don't get to the core of the issue. This important part of the Clearing Process is for returning to times of pain in your past, and using whatever methods are effective to let you re-experience the pain of that time. Let go of all understanding or analyzing. Just BE WITH how it was.

▶ **To feel it is to heal it. We will continue to be run by whatever we don't heal.**

ন্থ **Psychodrama is a very effective process. Put an empty chair in front of you and pretend that your parent, or other perpetrator is sitting in it. Then talk to them very strongly, speaking as the voice of the child you were, using swearing and yelling to get in touch more vividly with your feelings. Tell them in no uncertain terms what you needed.**

There is another effective form of Psychodrama.

ন্থ **Be the adult you are now and pretend you are holding the child you were in your** lap, listening to the pain, and hugging and encouraging that little self.

You did not have the words to talk back to your parents when you were very young, but you certainly had the feelings, and those are what you are putting words to now - the words you didn't have and could not say then.

႗ Remember how it is to be small and feel so intensely by spending time around kids if possible. Refer to the internet, or visit friends with small children. We forget how vulnerable and trusting and vehement little ones are - and we were! Get into your child mind.

We have to by-pass the intellect to hear our inner child's voice. The ego tries to save us from opening to the pain of the past by keeping us in the safer territory of THINKING about it all.

႗ Pretend to be a child again and that you are talking to a kind person who really wants to know what is happening to you, and is a good listener. Talk in a childish voice, using words that a very upset child would use, if only they had permission to feel and tell the truth, instead of having to repress it!

▶ The heart knows how to heal itself when we know how to listen to it.

ဆ Journaling is particularly effective for listening to yourself. It is an excellent way to reveal and explore your inner feelings. Writing also allows you to ground new awarenesses; they become stronger and more real when you write them down.

Another use of Journaling is to let your feelings flow naturally through free-writing, completing an open-ended phrase as though your child self was writing it; e.g. "I'm trying not to cry..."

Brendan Bays suggests, "Just don't move! Be completely present to the emotion. Don't do anything to distract yourself from it. Go right into the heart of it and discover what is at the core."

ဆ Use the third person approach.
Tell the story of your original experience by writing about it in your journal as though you are describing someone's else's life. This

sometimes allows you to more compassionately tell the truth about what really happened.

It is important that you don't overwhelm yourself in doing Clearing work. Only do it for limited periods of time; e.g. half an hour. And realize that it is not your whole self immersed in these painful episodes of your life. Only a part of you has the feelings Another part of you is being the witness.

▶ **The witness is your Spirit Self, which can never be touched or hurt by any human experience. It observes you from a space of total loving, confident in your work on the healing path.**

❧ **I picture my Witness Self as perched just above my right shoulder, nodding its head in approval as I re-experience my inner child's trauma.**

Involve your body in this feeling work. When you are re-experiencing pain, you may feel like your body wants to assume a specific position. For example, in the middle of one night while I was writing in my journal in the living room, my body wanted to lay on the floor in a fetal position. The very cells of your body will cooperate in your healing crisis, and inform you of what you want to remember.

▶ The body has its own wisdom.

CR Sing, draw or dance your feelings. It is known that music, art and movement provide avenues to connect with feelings. They bypass your ego/conscious mind, which sometimes tries to protect us from hurt by blocking access to the feelings.

Alice Miller advises that we must "say often and clearly, as much as is needed, what was done to us, until it is healed. Only then can we see that the whole world is not like our family; not a threat."

CR Use the breath! A child in trauma (or even an adult) tends to catch or hold their breath. If you will breathe frequently and a little more deeply while you are re-visiting your experience, it will facilitate emotional releasing.

Stillpoint Breathing, as taught by Michael Ryce, is an excellent technique for letting the body clear on its own, without needing to get specific about which particular stored emotion is releasing.

It consists of lying on the floor and doing connected breathing, deepening the breath a little more than usual, and keeping the rhythm steady, no matter what feelings or bodily sensations occur.

It is helpful to have a witness be with you, calmly encouraging a steady rhythm during your stillpoint breathing session. They should not get involved in your process, but only speak softly, facilitating your process.

ॐ Talk out loud to the Spiritual Self of your parent who has died.

If a parent has passed on, it is especially effective to do our healing with them! Expressing feelings to a parent who has died is hugely powerful.

You will have a sense of being heard, and especially of their ability to understand and parent you, perhaps unlike when they were alive. As a spiritual being, they now know the truth of the pain they helped you repress.

ॐ Use the Emotional Freedom Technique. (EFT)

This amazing process combines acupressure and the Clearing Process. It consists of repeated soft tapping on the meridians of the body, to clear blocked energy due to trauma, so that one does not have to repeat old negative behavior patterns. At the same time, one is led through a verbal process of total awareness and acceptance. I have been blessed to do this work with Hari Lubin hari@mcn.org and find it very effective to use for deeply getting in touch with the feelings around an issue.

▶ **Clearing can even sometimes happen suddenly!**

It can seem like we are not getting anywhere. We can spend days on feelings and feel stuck. If you stay with it however, the breakthrough can happen in a flash - from all the work you've already done.

Miriam Greenspan advises, "Being with a feeling in a state of awareness in which we don't avoid, cling to, try to fix, or try to understand, but are simply present; this is the process that makes the alchemy of a feeling (its transmutation) possible."

<u>Journal Experience:</u>

What I wanted to say, but could not when this happened to me as a child was...

Now my adult self would hold this child and tell her/him...

My Witness Spirit Self is telling me...

STEP 6: LIGHTEN UP - Bring in the light of Spirit

After a Clearing session, be sure to gain closure through invoking the light of Spirit. This work is difficult. It's important to support your self as you do it. At the end of each processing experience, visualize being bathed in the light; being lifted up and supported in peacefulness and joy.

Journal Experience:

As this pain clears way, and I open to the light I feel...

CHAPTER 10
Case Histories of Successful Clearing

An example of clearing shame:

Chris had been at a huge workshop and when she responded to a general question, the facilitator corrected what Chris said as though she didn't understand well enough. Everyone laughed at her! Chris was SO furious! Enraged! Her face felt so hot!

The incident stayed in her mind all day. She kept thinking of how rude he was and how embarrassed he had 'made her' and wishing she had never raised her hand to respond. She even tried to make light of it, and let it go, but she felt self-conscious around everyone there.

Later she realized that this was the perfect opportunity for the Clearing Process. (We had done some good healing work together in the past.) That evening in her hotel room she turned the lights low and lay down on the couch. She got in touch with the deep feelings. What came up was great embarrassment and anger at not being respected.

She asked herself when she'd felt those exact feelings in the past. She thought of when she had felt the same way while cocktail waitressing in her twenties; the other waitresses had treated her as though was a naive young girl, even though she had certainly 'been around' and had been doing that work for several years already!

Then she remembered feeling very excluded when she joined a tennis club in her thirties. She just didn't know how to socialize easily, and never could think of how to take part when the other gals were joking around; they were so easy-going with each other.

Then the horrible weekend when she went to a three-day retreat and ended up not having anyone to hang out with the whole time came to mind. That had been such a lonely time; she felt like everyone noticed that she was 'not good enough' to even make any friends.

The earliest times she recalled were in elementary school when the other kids would laugh at her, and she felt very much excluded year after year.

The worst incident she remembered was the time in third grade when they were supposed to sit quietly with their heads on their arms on the desks. She dropped her sweater and reached down on the floor. The child designated as monitor reported her. The teacher had said that any child who was then reported would get their finger pricked with a needle.

When the teacher returned Chris was taken into another room. No finger-pricking happened but she started crying in front of everyone. She was SO embarrassed! It seemed like the entire class made fun of her for days afterward.

Chris now realized that her intense over-reaction to the seminar facilitator's response was her own stuff. If she had not had this readiness to feel embarrassed and shamed, she would have been able to laugh at herself along with the other folks who were actually well-meaning and in support of her. She realized that the embarrassment at the weekend seminar was a perfect, God-given doorway to healing that old shame.

She stayed with the feelings of her little girl self; remembering the horrible shame of having to stand and be led out of the room by the teacher, with all of the other kids laughing at her. She kept breathing steadily, letting the feelings intensify. She let her face get hotter and hotter and cried about how awful it felt to be friendless and alone.

For the next few days, she let the feelings come up, returning to the old experience as often as she remembered. She even imagined what she would have said to that teacher and the other kids, if she'd had the courage.

Finally, she knew it was done! She was finished with the shame she had been holding all those years. Chris subsequently noticed that she began to feel much more at ease in social situations, and over the years since, she has effortlessly become involved in wonderful friendships.

An example of clearing disgust:

Mark was frustrated because whenever he went out of town with his friends from work he actually did not have a good time. He wanted to fit in with them, since they had to see each other so much anyway on the job, but found that he was frequently preferring to stay by himself at the hotel and read, or even go off to sightsee on his own.

He kept trying to make himself hang out and party with them, but when he did he kept thinking about how much he didn't like them. Still, he wasn't comfortable just making an excuse and leaving; he didn't know what to say!

When we went into the first step of doing the Clearing process together (awareness and acceptance) what came up for Mark was disgust and contempt for 'those people.' An analogy that captured how he felt was of himself up in a tower spitting down onto his friends standing below, while they were oblivious of him.

He felt the intense emotions in his throat, and he said it was like a rigid rod stuck there. As he looked at it more, he said it seemed like a cinnamon stick was lodged in his throat.

We began to explore other times and places in his life when he also had withdrawn from social opportunities because of dislike for the people involved. He saw how when he'd had a restaurant for years, he was obligated to fraternize with the customers and how he'd resented the time he had to spend with them.

He recalled how he hated playing cards with his first wife's friends every Friday evening, but condescended to do so to keep peace in the marriage.

Mark began to see that this situation with his friends was just another incident in a pattern in his life. He had experienced this contempt in other important situations.

He was then able to let go of thinking his dislike of his friends was because of how they were; to let go of blaming his feelings on them. He owned the experience as somehow being set up by himself - or rather by his deeper Self to get his attention for healing something.

As Mark opened further to the intense feelings of disgust and resentment, it became apparent that he had felt that same way as a young child too.

Whenever his parents had been entertaining guests at home and drinking, they eventually woke him up late at night to come out to the living room and show off. His dad and he often played number games on car trips, and he had enjoyed the fun of it.

But when they woke him, his father would cajole him into demonstrating how he could figure out large sums in his head and perform other mental arithmetic tricks. Mark was three or four years old at the time. He was applauded and hugged and kissed by people who were disgusting and drunk!

Mark was especially able to get in touch with his anger when I asked him to sketch the scene as he imagined it. His compassion for that little boy was touching.

He also had a powerful experience of talking out loud to his parents about how resentful he was for their making him be nice when he hated being around those 'awful people.'

Subsequently Mark realized that he did not want to spend time with those particular friends outside of work. He was able to easily let them know that he was otherwise committed when they invited him to go. While at first they teased him and asked what was wrong, they were soon able to accept his unavailability on weekends, and his work environment did not suffer at all.

Mark finally realized that he had been unconsciously forcing himself to go against his own preferences in order to have the opportunity to heal these old wounds.

An example of clearing anger:

I was so worried about my mom! She lived a couple of hours from me in Lakeland, Florida, and I had been notified that she'd been taken into the hospital.

Apparently she had not been eating and her electrolytes were imbalanced. The worst thing was that, when I visited her there, I was informed that she had been violent with the hospital staff and they were considering placing her in the 6th floor psych ward. They were not optimistic.

I talked with my mom, trying to find out the problem; why she was acting so violently. She replied that she didn't want to get better.

She wanted to die. My dad had passed on a few months before, and she said that she felt like she now had nothing to live for.

Apparently she had 'forgotten' all of the abuse she received from him, and how much she had wanted to be free of him when he was still alive. Now she only spoke of how happy they had been, and she certainly did not want to be reminded otherwise by me!

I was quite discouraged and during the three hour drive home, I found myself in tears. As I opened to the deeper feelings underlying my sadness I realized I had huge rage. It was not at my mom or the hospital; rather it was at my dad. It wasn't because he had died either. I started looking at the times in my young life and childhood when I might have felt that intense anger and not been able to get in touch with it.

I began imagining how it must have been when he had left my mom alone with three little girls and no money for food, as I had heard he did so many times. And I recalled her tears when he would lose job after job because of his drinking. And I asked myself what was under the fear I'd had when he hit her so many times over the years, and realized my rage about it.

I started talking out loud to my dad's spirit in the car; yelling and swearing and saying to him how I knew he could hear me now and understand, and I was so furious for all the things he had done to my mom. I talked about the things he had done to us girls too and how furious I was at how badly he had acted as a father.

As I arrived home, I felt exhausted, but clear, knowing that I had done some good clearing of my old woundedness. Because of my past experience with emotional healing work, I knew it would benefit me greatly; however even I was surprised and delighted at the next development.

When I traveled to Lakeland Hospital the next time, I was told that my mom had done a turn-around. She had become settled and peaceful, and was also physically recovered enough to go home.

I asked my mom what had happened. She said that she had realized that my dad would want her to keep on living; that he had given her a lot of hard times in her life, and that now he would be happy if she let herself be happy.

I felt tears on my face as I silently whispered "thank you God." What I knew inside was that as I healed my anger, I no longer needed to have anyone provide me with reason to feel it. And, as I released myself from my stuck emotion, I inadvertently also released my mother from hers. Our lives were free to shift.

PART III

The Clearing Process and You

If you are considering using this process for your own healing, there are several options.

You may choose to work by yourself, using this text as your guidebook. That can be a challenging choice, since we tend to want to move too quickly through our own issues when we are working alone. If you choose this option, it will be extremely helpful to acquire "The Clearing Process Workbook." The Workbook will lead you step by step through each phase of your personal transformation.

Alternatively you can contact and employ the help of a therapist. In Part III, you will find several suggestions that involve a combination of both approaches, as well as information to help you make a decision to begin your healing.

We'll consider the benefits people have described experiencing as a result of doing this clearing work, and conclude with an overview of what you might encounter in beginning the Clearing Process.

CHAPTER 11
How you May Expect to Benefit from the Clearing Process

Following a Clearing Process, wonderful changes will become evident in you. Have an expectation of great good as a result of the healing work you have successfully allowed in yourself.

▶ When you have cleared an old emotion, either of three things will happen:

1) The situation that bothered you will change significantly.
2) The situation may stay the same, but it won't bother you. You have cleared that feeling.
3) You will easily end the situation, since you are done with its influence in your life.

▶ The ramifications of your healing work may be surprising. The psychic energy that was tied up in keeping old emotions unconscious is now free for creative and joyful living.

▶ Physical conditions that used to bother you will vanish. There is so much evidence that the body is adversely affected by emotional baggage. You will deal with issues before they show up in your body.

▶ Healing is a cumulative process. As you continue to use clearing, you are learning healthy self-therapy. Each time you do it, it gets easier and heals more quickly. Eventually you will be able to do clearing right in the moment of an interaction with a loved one; you will naturally do the process within yourself. You will get to a point where just consciously becoming aware of an old emotional reaction to someone in your present experience is enough to dissolve the toxic psychic energy further.

▶ In your relationships, you will be able witness for another without taking responsibility for them. You can be with your feelings authentically in intimate encounters, holding steady your love for the other person. You can allow them their own feelings, and you yours, without needing to try to make anything in particular happen.

▶ Clarity comes after you've done the work. Once you no longer have a heavy emotional response to something, you will easily explore how to handle it; i.e. what to do; what feels right. Clarity comes automatically when the emotion is dissipated.

▶ Life changes when your vibration changes. Everything unfolds naturally when you have done your clearing work. People will start acting differently toward you. Things that bothered you before no longer do.

▶ As you continue to stay in touch with your present-moment feelings, you will discover a confidence in handling whatever occurs in your life. Because you own your issues, you will not get stuck in blame and victimhood. You will be able to use the Clearing Process to deal with whatever uncomfortable feelings come up.

CHAPTER 12
Entering the Clearing Process

The following information will serve to help you decide whether to work directly with us at The Clearing Process...for Conscious Living

Our practice is physically located in San Rafael, California. To arrange an in-person interview, you will find contact information available at www.clearingprocess.com. However many of our Clearing Process clients live out of the area. They are supported by using interactive computer video; either Skype or Face Time. This way of working together has proven to be just as effective as in-person sessions.

And it is always so much fun and a joy to later meet in person those clients whom we have come to know so intimately over cyberspace. We feel like old friends hugging for the first time!

Individual therapy unfolds as outlined above in Chapter 9 - The Clearing Process. In order to provide your therapist with as much helpful information as possible, after the first session you will be invited to complete a form which will provide an outline of your personal history. Information requested will include a description of any significant issues in your parents' and grandparents' lives, as well as your personal story.

The length of therapy varies greatly from person to person. Since this Clearing Process guidebook will be provided to you in the beginning, you will have the advantage of a roadmap to follow. Therefore, only a few sessions may be needed to support you in your Clearing Process.

On the other hand, some people choose to continue their emotional healing by keeping the assistance of a supportive personal therapist. As each issue from the past is uncovered and cleared, they develop greater and greater ability to live consciously.

Others work with a therapist for a few sessions, and then check in periodically as needed. This approach seems to work the best! You and your therapist have already established an intimate bond, which makes further work together, on an as-needed basis, really effective.

This format for emotional transformation is also exciting because it becomes obvious over a period of time how well you are learning the Clearing Process as self-therapy. You become able to more and more quickly resolve issues that come up.

In personal one-on-one therapy, the sessions are recorded and the CD given to you, with instructions to listen to it in full before your next appointment. So much healing work is accomplished in each session, and it becomes more deeply grounded if you can hear it again by yourself. For this reason, clients whose therapy is online are also encouraged to record the sessions for later listening.

You will be invited to share photographs from your early life. The discussion during reviewing these together is often poignant and lends immeasurably to the therapist's intuitive awareness of your personal healing journey.

Another effective contribution to the Clearing Process is for you to read aloud to your therapist insights and experiences you have written in your journal between sessions.

If you choose to be your own Clearing Process therapist, first of all purchase The Clearing Process Workbook. It will greatly assist you as a step-by-step companion to this Guidebook. It will make the personal work come alive for you.

Also, read from the books mentioned in Chapter Six. The works of Alice Miller and J. Konrad Stettbacher are especially valuable for heightening your awareness of the power of childhood repression in attracting your present situation. Very few people are aware of how our subliminal vibration literally creates our experience in the world.

CHAPTER 13
Group Work

Individual therapy has become a pre-requisite for participation in Clearing Process groups. Both online and in-person groups contain no more than two to five members.

The intention is not for personal advice-giving between clients. The best format for the group is for participants to listen while each individual works with the therapist. This phenomenon is sometimes referred to as 'borrowing benefits.' Hearing others' issues also allows each person to realize how unique and personal their own history is.

Being part of a group is contingent on your having reached essential insights in your own healing journey.

It is also required that you make a commitment to confidentiality and to respect others in your group.

CONCLUSION

The Clearing Process is without a doubt the most effective approach I've yet experienced for living consciously.

After all the years of counseling education and research; after all of the therapists I used and clients I helped; after all of the books I read and the techniques I investigated, I find that feeling deeply and telling the whole truth about it, without blaming anyone in our present life, is the most powerful pathway.

Life gets better and better. We are blessed with joy, love, health and the excitement of living divinely inspired purpose!